Our American Family™

I Am Indian American

Jane Stuart

The Rosen Publishing Group's
PowerKids Press™
New York

Published in 1997 by The Rosen Publishing Group, Inc.
29 East 21st Street, New York, NY 10010

Copyright © 1997 by The Rosen Publishing Group, Inc.

First Edition

Book Design: Erin McKenna

Photo Credits: Cover © James Davis/International Stock Photo; p. 4 © Ron Rovtar/FPG International Corp.; p. 7 © Frank Grant/International Stock Photo; p. 8 © Phyllis Picardi/International Stock Photo; p. 11 © FPG International Corp.; p. 15 © Julian Calder/International Stock Photo; p. 16 © Johnny Stockshooter/International Stock Photo; p. 19 © Miwako Ikeda/International Stock Photo; p. 20 © Tom O'Brien/International Stock Photo.

Stuart, Jane.
   I am Indian American / by Jane Stuart.
      p.   cm. — (Our American Family)
  Includes index.
  Summary: Briefly discusses an Indian's heritage, including clothes, food, holidays, and religion.
  ISBN 0-8239-5008-5
  1. Indian Americans—Social life and customs—Juvenile literature. 2. India—Social life and customs—Juvenile literature. 3. United States—Social life and customs—Juvenile literature.
  [1. Indian Americans.] I. Title. II. Series.
E184.E2S78 1997
973'.04914—dc21   96-40530
                                           CIP
                                           AC

Manufactured in the United States of America

Contents

Karim

My name is Karim. My grandparents came to America from New Delhi, which is the capital of India. I live with my mom, dad, and grandfather in New York City. My grandfather loves to show me pictures of New Delhi. He also tells me stories about India. He wants to make sure I never forget where my family came from.

◀ You can learn about your family history by talking to your parents or relatives.

5

Where Is India?

In 1492, Christopher Columbus sailed from Spain to find a country called India. It was a very long trip. When his ships finally landed, he thought he had found what he was looking for. He even called the people he met "Indians." But Columbus had actually landed in North America by mistake. India, the country he was searching for, is halfway around the world on a **continent** (KON-tin-ent) called Asia.

India has a long and colorful history. Part of its history includes the Taj Mahal, ▶ which is a memorial in Agra.

A Better Life

India is more crowded than almost any other country in the world. There are more than 9 million people in India! Because of this, many don't have a place to live or enough food to eat. Most Indians believe that animals are as important as humans. They would never kill a cow for food because cows are sacred, or holy, animals in India. My grandparents got tired of struggling every day. They left India because they believed they could have a better life in America.

◀ Many of India's cities and villages are overcrowded.

An Indian Hero

My grandfather has a picture of **Mohandas Gandhi** (moh-HAN-dahs GAHN-dee) hanging in his room. Gandhi saw all the troubles in India and wanted to help. He knew that part of the problem was that the British controlled the Indian government. He led the Indian people in a fight for **independence** (IN-dee-PEN-dents). Unlike other wartime leaders, he led a peaceful **protest** (PRO-test). Sadly, Gandhi was killed in 1948, the year after India gained its freedom.

10

Gandhi is still considered a hero all over the world. ▶

Hinduism

My family is **Hindu** (HIN-doo). That means we practice a very old religion called **Hinduism** (HIN-doo-izm). Most Hindus believe there are many gods. Each god has a special meaning or power.

Two of the most important Hindu gods are named Vishnu and Shiva. My family prays to them in a beautiful temple painted in bright colors. The top of the temple is decorated with statues and drawings of many gods and goddesses.

◄ Temples are an important part of a Hindu's religion. Hindus often work together to repair them.

13

Other Indian Religions

Most Indians are Hindus. However, there are also Indian Christians, Muslims, and Jews. In addition, some Indians are **Buddhists** (BOOD-ists). Hindus, Buddhists, and members of a religion called **Jainism** (JY-nizm) follow the idea that all living things should be treated with respect. The smallest animal is as important as the biggest. My grandfather says that it's wrong even to kill a spider.

14

There are many different religions practiced in India. These Muslims, who follow the religion of Islam, pray every day at the same time. ▶

Diwali

Every November my family celebrates a holiday called **Diwali** (dee-VAL-ee), or The Festival of Lights. *Diwali* is the start of the Hindu New Year. We light many oil-filled lamps and pray to the goddess Lakshmi for a good year. My parents give me toys, and my grandfather gives me candy. In India, kids light firecrackers and families keep their lamps lit all night long. During *Diwali* the whole country seems to glow.

◀ Temples that were built in honor of the goddess Lakshmi can be found all over India.

17

Saris

My mother wears a dress called a **sari** (SAR-ee). A sari is one big piece of cloth that is folded in a special way. The fabric is draped over one shoulder and falls to my mother's feet, so most of her body is covered. Saris come in lots of colors and are decorated with beautiful patterns. My mother also paints a dot called a bindi in the middle of her forehead. The bindi means different things to the different people who wear it. Many women wear it as a sign of beauty.

18

Indian women often wear part of their saris over their heads. ▶

Food

Most Indians eat a kind of flat bread called **roti** (ROH-tee). My mother bakes a type of roti called **chapatti** (chu-PAHT-ee) in the oven. We eat roti with rice and vegetable dishes. Everyone in my family is a **vegetarian** (vej-eh-TAYR-ee-un). That means that we don't eat meat. My favorite dish is *palak paneer*. It's made with spinach and cheese.

Indian food is cooked with a lot of different spices, such as cumin and green chiles.

◀ Some Indian dishes use meat as well as vegetables, such as this curried chicken and vegetables dish.

21

I Am Indian American

My parents want me to understand what's special about being both Indian and American. I learn about the United States in school, and my grandpa tells me all about the history and traditions of India. I'm glad I know about two great countries. I am proud to be a part of both of them.

22

Glossary

Buddhist (BOOD-ist) A person who practices a religion called Buddhism.

continent (KON-tin-ent) A very large area of land.

chapatti (chu-PAHT-ee) A type of Indian bread.

Diwali (dee-VAL-ee) The Festival of Lights that is held in celebration of the Hindu New Year.

Mohandas Gandhi (moh-HAN-dahs GAHN-dee) The peaceful leader who helped Indians gain their freedom from the British.

Hindu (HIN-doo) A person who practices Hinduism.

Hinduism (HIN-doo-izm) A religion that started in India and is practiced by people all over the world.

independence (IN-dee-PEN-dents) Freedom of a country to rule itself.

Jainism (JY-nizm) A religion whose followers believe in the respect for all living things.

protest (PRO-test) To show that you object to or disapprove of something.

roti (ROH-tee) Indian flat bread.

sari (SAR-ee) A long, colorful dress worn by Indian women.

vegetarian (vej-eh-TAYR-ee-un) A person who doesn't eat meat.

23

Index